An Awesome Meal

Chapter 5
Lesson 86: Special Vowel Sounds *AU/AW*
Lexile® Measure: 420L

Printed in the United States of America

Copyright © September 2012 by Reading Horizons

No part of this publication may be reproduced, stored in a retrieval system, or transmitted in any form or by any means, electronic, mechanical, photocopying, recording, or otherwise, without the prior permission of the copyright owner.

ISBN 978-1-62382-041-1

"What is that awful smell?" Austin asked with a yawn. He sauntered into the kitchen. His mother was standing at the stove. She was looking at their morning meal.

"I accidentally burned the toast. I also dropped the sausage. Then, I scorched the applesauce!" she cried. "Maybe we should hire someone to fix our meals. I am not very good at this. I am better at doing the laundry."

Austin and his mother sat down at the table. They wrote an advertisement for some help. This is what it said:

> *Wanted: Someone to fix awesome meals! We will provide the food if you will fix the meals. It must taste good. Please apply at the stone cottage on Maple Street. Ask for Austin.*

The next day, Austin and his mother were reading by the fireplace. There was a knock on their door. His mother quickly opened the door. She saw a tall man. He was holding the hand of a scrawny, little girl.

"Good day," said the man as he tipped his hat. "My name is Paul. This is my daughter. Her name is Audra. We are here to respond to your advertisement. I can fix meals that taste very good. You will not need to pay me if my daughter and I can stay in your barn. Will you hire me to fix your meals?"

Austin showed Paul the kitchen and the pantry full of food. Paul pulled some pots and pans out of his knapsack. He began to make the food into a meal. After a while, Austin could smell something amazing coming from the kitchen.

"Come and eat," called Paul.

Austin saw a lot of food on the table. He saw mashed potatoes, hot rolls, and creamy applesauce. He saw juicy sausage and roasted beef.

"This looks like a fine feast!" said Austin.

They all sat down to eat the awesome meal. As Austin smacked his lips in delight, he told Paul and Audra they could live with them as long as they wanted.

The End

Comprehension Questions

1. What was the main problem in this story?
    a. Austin and his mother needed a cook.
    b. Paul was a better cook than Austin's mom.
    c. Austin and his mom did not have a pan with which to cook.

2. What did Paul want if he agreed to cook for Austin and his mother?
    a. He didn't want anything.
    b. He wanted five dollars a day.
    c. He wanted to live in the barn.

3. Paul came to Austin and his mother to respond to their advertisement. When you *respond* to someone, you
    a. ignore them.
    b. call to say hello.
    c. give them an answer or reply.

4. Did Austin like the food that Paul cooked?
   a. Yes
   b. No

5. After reading the story, what would you guess was true about Paul and Audra?
   a. They were not very rich.
   b. They lived in a nice house.
   c. They had plenty of food to eat.

Skill Words

applesauce	awful	sauntered	yawn
Audra	daughter	sausage	
Austin	laundry	saw	
awesome	Paul	scrawny	

Most Common Words

a	he	need	to
after	help	next	very
all	her	not	wanted
also	here	of	was
an	his	on	we
are	I	opened	were
as	if	our	what
ask	into	out	while
asked	is	reading	will
at	it	said	with
by	like	saw	you
called	little	she	your
can	live	should	
come	long	showed	
could	looking	some	
day	looks	something	
doing	make	that	
down	man	the	
food	me	their	
for	mother	them	
from	must	then	
good	my	there	
hand	name	they	

Challenge Words

door	daughter